VANISHING JAPAN

VANISHING JAPAN

BY MORTON WESLEY HUBER

A Glimpse of an Ancient Land in Photographs, Watercolors, Ink and Pencil Sketches ✽ *Decorative Lettering by Kyoko Huber.*

CHILTON BOOKS   *A Division of Chilton Company, Publishers*   *Philadelphia*

AMPHOTO   *American Photographic Book Publishing Co., Inc.*   *New York*

TO MY WIFE

whose devotion and understanding
are a constant source of inspiration

LIST OF ILLUSTRATIONS

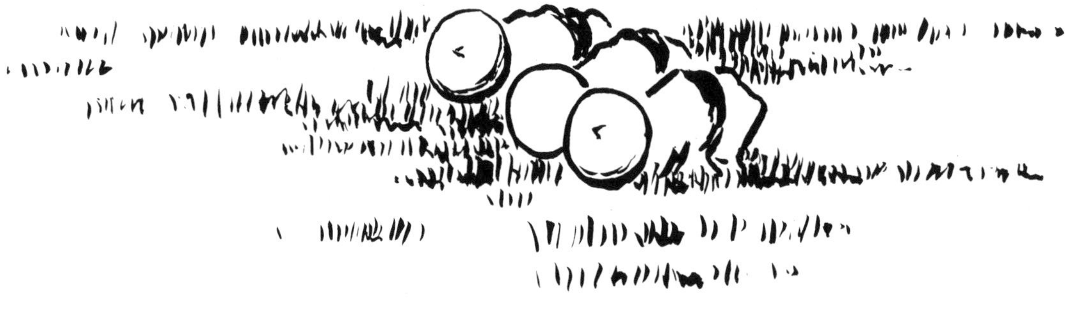

Introduction

Long centuries ago, when the world was a shadowy mist, the Islands of Japan were born of the sea. Among the many gods inhabiting this misty abode were Izanagi and Izanami. One day, while they were standing on the Floating Bridge of Heaven, talking with each other, Izanagi said: "I wonder what is down below us?" This aroused Izanami's curiosity, and they began to think how they might find out. Taking the Jewel-Spear of Heaven, Izanagi lowered it into the air and swung it around in an effort to strike something, for he could not see through the dense mist. Suddenly the spear touched the ocean. When Izanagi raised it, salty water dripping from it was dried by the wind, becoming hard, and forming an island in the middle of the sea.

"Let us go down and live on the island," said Izanagi. And so they descended from the Floating Bridge of Heaven to live on the island. Soon they had created the Great-Eight-Island-Land and given

9

birth to three noble children: the Sun Goddess and her brothers the Moon God and the Storm God. The Sun Goddess, whose name was Amaterasu-Omi-Kami, also had a family. Her grandson Jimmu became the first Emperor (Tenno or Mikado) of Japan.

From the sea rose great mountains belching fire, while here and there on the islands were steaming, bubbling pools of restless brimstone. The mightiest peak of all, looking far out over the Pacific, is Fujiyama, Japan's sacred mountain. Guardian of the islands, Fuji is visible for 60 miles in clear weather.

The origin of Japan is recorded in the oldest scripture, the *Kojiki* (Records of Ancient Matters), which achieved written form in the early part of the eighth century. Shintoism, Japan's native religion, teaches that the emperor is descended from the gods. Even the Japanese flag displays the red circle for the Land of the Rising Sun, where once lived the Sun Goddess Amaterasu.

The 12,000 foot peak of Mt. Fuji photographed from the
volcanic shores of Enoshima Island, 43 miles distant.

Scientifically, the origin of the Japanese people is
still in dispute. The race is, however, compounded
of elements drawn from various parts of Asia
in prehistoric times. In the Neolithic period
Mongol tribes arrived from Korea. Others came
from South China and possibly from Polynesia. The
Ainu, now inhabiting Hokkaido, at one time spread

古事記より

over the whole archipelago. This latter race is of Caucasian rather than Oriental origin.

Though Japan is an ancient country to the western world, she is chronologically young in Asia. This land was an unexplored group of islands inhabited by savage clans, when India's advanced culture had already given the world such important names as Prince Mahavira and Prince Gautama, the Buddha. In China an advanced civilization had bloomed for centuries. The Chinese had already produced exquisite art and literature and had made strides in science and government when the primitive people of Japan still lived by simple methods of hunting and fishing.

Today the story is quite different. Busy cities hum where jinrikisha wheels once turned in the mud. Each year scores of visitors roam the shores of the land that had remained closed to the outside

人力車

world until, in 1854, Commodore Perry steamed into Tokyo Bay. Save for the stories of a few missionaries, our first-hand knowledge of Japan dates back little more than a century. But rapid change began at once, for an antiquated political and social order was suddenly exposed to the far advanced civilizations of Europe and America.

The long isolation of Japan from the rest of the world, combined with Shinto teachings, was responsible for the fanatically strong nationalistic spirit of the Japanese. Shintoism became a militant religion. Schoolchildren learned that their most important deeds would be those done for the emperor and the glory of Japan. Even foreign conquest in the name of the emperor was justified, for he was descended from the gods, and the Japanese people were destined to rule the earth. To look upon the emperor meant blindness, and to touch his divine being meant death.

13

In armed conflict first with China and then Russia, Japan fared remarkably well. With the army gradually slipping from the emperor's control into the hands of the war lords, it was almost inevitable that this growing fiery nationalism should erupt into the attack on Pearl Harbor, on December 7th, 1941.

Total defeat in World War II brought sweeping changes again, this time by United States post-war occupation. Westernization and modernization were rapid. The larger cities have lost much of their mystery and flavor. They are centers of jet transportation, mass production methods, and business by electronics.

With help from the United States, the Japanese economy has grown phenomenally. All tillable land is under cultivation, and the yield per acre is so good that overall farm production is up 40%. The long-established diet of rice, beans, and fish is gradually being supplemented by better vegetables,

meats, and dairy products. In 1953 Japan was importing one million tons of rice annually, but today she is self-sufficient in this product.

In rate of growth of her gross national product, Japan leads all the nations. She ranks first in shipbuilding and third in the production of steel. This is indeed remarkable for a nation starting anew after the ravages of war, whose total land area is no greater than the State of California. Her close neighbor, Red China, whose regimented communes and forced labor are yielding unsatisfactory results, presents a startling contrast.

In the midst of all this rapid change, where is the Japan of old? Where are the quaint inns and tea houses, the lovely gardens that once flourished here? Is the door to the past sealed forever? Ghostly and elusive are the echoes of a day that has sped into eternity. Yet the centuries turn back for those who would hear her feeble call, for those

水蓮の池

who would seek her haunting caress. Marks etched by the past are not so easily erased.

In rural areas where ancient customs still prevail, Japan is richest in tradition. A lonely pine-clad shore, a pair of wooden shoes by a thatch-roofed house, a quiet pagoda silhouetted against the sky, ever-changing abstract reflections in a lotus pond—the door is near at hand. (*Color plates* 1 *and* 2.) City noises fade into silence. Old Fuji rumbles and belches smoke, as if resenting the disturbance of her sleep by travellers from another age.

But alas, each of us sees only what he wants to see—or perhaps more correctly, what he has trained himself to see—and among all those who pass this way, only a few will find old Japan. The key to turning back time depends upon a few ingredients for which there is no substitute: a bit of simple love, a generous pinch of feeling, and a full measure of imagination.

18

Vanishing Japan

In the quiet of the morning, when cherry petals are still wet with dew, a Buddhist priest chants his early prayer. A chipmunk stops to peep, then scurries on. Ghostly gray pines climb into the mist on a nearby mountain slope; moss-covered forest paths catch the rays of a still pale morning sun. Bamboo trees sway gently in the wakening breeze, and there, in a forest clearing, stands an ancient weather-worn *torii* fashioned by skilled hands long since passed back to dust. Beside it, a broken stone altar crumbles away into sand. Once this lonely grove knew the anxious steps of those whose innermost wishes and urgent pleas sought the Buddha.

Now a low and penetrating gong is carried on the still morning air. It comes from a small building standing in the temple garden. This building is the belfry, housing an immense bronze bell. With every

The sweet scent of pines
on a fresh morning breeze.

22

鐘つき男

muscle taut, the bell ringer strains to move a heavy wooden striker in its cradle. The bell is rung on the hour; its low sound carries for miles across the city. Traditionally these bells are struck 108 times on New Year's Eve to absolve the populace of each of man's 108 sins. The largest bell in Japan was cast in 1633 and is housed on the grounds of Chion-in Temple in Kyoto. This giant weighs 74 tons and requires a team of men to ring it. The great bell at Todaiji in Nara was cast in 733; for more than 12 centuries its low tones have summoned the faithful to prayer.

As the day grows older, street vendors begin to hawk their wares. The vendors are women as often as men, frequently pulling carts unbelievably large (*Color plates* 3.) Goods for sale include foods and household items of every description. One stand has no wheels and is carried by a peddler who has a curious collection of wind bells for sale.

Where once a Shinto altar stood
stout bamboos now flourish.

Bell ringer. ▷

Mountain road near Ohara.

Street vendor.

風鈴りん

Made of thin pieces of glass, they tinkle softly as he walks. By the side of the road stand wagons with doors folded down and locked. They are open for business in the evenings, offering noodles and soup for sale. Still other vendors with lantern-decorated wagons sell *yakitori*, a kind of shishkabob. Pieces of chicken meat and liver arranged on a stick are toasted over an open flame. Laborers returning home crowd these stands, where they pause for a glass of *sake* and some yakitori.

On many street corners, women bootblacks earn a meager living. In the parks, women rake leaves and clean the streets. (*Color plate 5.*) Along quiet country roads they pull carts laden with bales of hay. The slow clopping of sandals against sun-baked soil echoes down through the long centuries. Winding mountain roads have known the tread of strong young feet and marked the slow but certain change of feeble steps that one day passed forever.

28

Wind bells. ▲

The Japanese characters on the following page are freely translated as follows: The moon is hidden from view by a dark sky. Chill rain penetrates deep, deep to the bone as this aged woman moves with feeble steps. ▷

お月さまかくれ

老の身にしみいる

冬の雨

◁ Solitary planter working among young rice plants at Niwase. Far in the distance mountains jut abruptly from the plain.

Only 60 miles from Tokyo, the farm village of Karasawa retains its ancient appearance with thatched roofs and narrow dirt roads where heavy carts bump along over jagged stones.

田植うた

Window to the past— ▷
At daybreak, beside a quiet stream in Niwase,
the day's work begins.

Drops of water between the reeds, ripples on a quiet pool, a figure crouched as aged hands pound clothes upon the rocks and wring them with determined grip—the ancient chore of washing clothes in a river goes on regularly in the farmlands. Modern washing machines are rare, and families that can afford them are rarer still. Women do a large share of the manual labor. Sorely-bent figures of aged women whose backs will never again straighten are the result of a lifetime in the rice fields. Through the long daylight hours, the workers bend as industrious fingers set each tender plant. The task is slow; there is little mechanization.

In the rice lands, houses, barns, and other buildings are erected in groups, on mounds of dry land surrounded by the flooded fields. The distance between these hamlets may be a mile or two. Far

34

△ Farm houses at Ohara, near Kyoto.

◁ A lone farmer works late—Niwase.

A quiet summer's day — Nakasho.

The old boat — Niwase. ▷

Home in the rice lands—Niwase.

41

into the distance, rice plants stand in neat rows. (*Color plates* 6, 7). As the season moves along, the watery world seems to disappear, for the plants grow tall and obscure their bases. Rolling hills are a rarity in Japan. Volcanic action has formed a landscape where steep hills and rugged mountains lift their heads directly from the flat plateaus. All tillable areas are utilized—no land is wasted. Each hamlet has vegetable plots laid out between the several buildings. Coarse mats stretched out on the ground are covered with beans drying in the sun. Like plucked chickens in a meat market, onions are strung from ropes hung under the eaves of the houses. (*Color plates* 8, 9, 10 *and* 11.) Living quarters are tidy and clean, for cleanliness is a virtue of the Japanese people in general. Although the greater number of buildings have tiled roofs, the thatched roof is still a familiar sight. Often as thick as two feet, it keeps the interior quite dry even during the rainy season.

わらはこび

Rain, the lonely ▷
village road.

Some crops, such as tea, can be grown on steep hillsides. Green tea, popular here, has a bitter taste to the novice. It is prepared by drying the leaves directly instead of steaming them. A tall grass called *igusa* is another product peculiar to this part of the world. It grows to a length of five feet and, after being cut and dried, it can easily be woven into mats. These soft *tatami* mats, two to three inches thick, cover the floors of home, temple, and *ryokan*. As is the custom, shoes are removed before walking upon them.

Rainy season transforms the rice lands into a sea of mud. Popular travel by motorcycle and bicycle is difficult. Children returning home from school sink ankle deep in the oozing mud. The long way home becomes even longer as night spreads a foggy cloak over flooded fields. (*Color plates* 12, 13 *and* 14.) The farm lands are indeed Japan, for through her long history she has depended upon a rice economy.

Today she is many things. She is the summit

44

of Fuji drifting silently in a sea of clouds, an
ancient temple garden flecked with newly fallen
cherry petals, the sound of great new industries in
birth. But most of all, Japan is the people. They
are both the past and the future. They reflect the
world of yesterday, yet provide a glimpse of what
is to come. A fascinating culture is their legacy,
the Japan of tomorrow their responsibility.

45

火鉢の時代

Though history records the deeds of these people, an examination of Japanese art and literature opens up the heart. The motivation for art is the deepest of emotions. The expression is truthful, for it has little reason to be otherwise. A keen and sensitive love of nature permeates this work. The murmur of a secluded brook is made to sing forever in the simplest of written lines. A minimum of skillful strokes characterizes its subtle water-colors. Mountains rising from the mist are made a deep and personal experience.

One soon learns that differences in physical appearance are not necessarily accompanied by an altered emotional or psychological make-up. These people feel the same love, the same pain, and the same needs as others the world over. But linked by custom and tradition to a somewhat different social order, their view of the world that lies before them is not the same as that of the

46

westerner. The Japanese are an energetic people, full of curiosity, and with a passion for learning that is second only to their love of nature. Industry and government have been quick to borrow from the best examples throughout the world. Competition for entrance to Japanese universities is keen.

The hearts and minds of the older people belong to their ancestors. Ties with the past are strong; the minds of the aged live on memories. (*Color plate* 21.) They knew a time when outsiders were never seen on their shores—a time when the wealth of the nation belonged to a few, and the masses worked as laborers for rich overlords. They have seen the Empire at its greatest glory, and have suffered the shock and humiliation of total defeat. They live in a changing world, but cling to the habits and customs of yesterday. The charcoal *hibachi* cooks their food and takes the chill away when the world

48

Plate 1   Wind-blown pines high above the Pacific—Aburatsubo.

Plate 2   Ancient pagoda in a forest clearing—Kyoto. ▶

Plate 3   Her simple trade—Tokyo.

Plate 4   Through the long summer's heat.

Plate 5   Street cleaners—Tokyo.

Plate 6
Gray skies over Niwase.

Plate 7   *On a quiet morning—Niwase.*

Plate 8   Filling rice sacks—Niwase.

Plate 9   Early riser—Niwase.

Plate 10   Beside the lazy canal—Niwase.

Plate 11   *Off to school—Niwase.*

Plate 13   Enoshima.

◀ Plate 12   The toilers—near Hakone.

Plate 14   Rainy season—Fujisawa.

Fujisawa, Japan

Plate 15   *The main square—Fujisawa.*

Plates 16, 17
Wielding a long stick, the blindfolded contestant searches for the watermelon.

Plate 18
Shinto priests on a hot day file beneath a large sign that advertises a favorite dish, vinegared rice—Kamakura.

Plate 19
Aisatsu—greetings on a Sunday afternoon—Kamakura.

Plate 20   *Scrolls for sale—Kamakura.*

Pine-clad hills — Inamuragasaki.

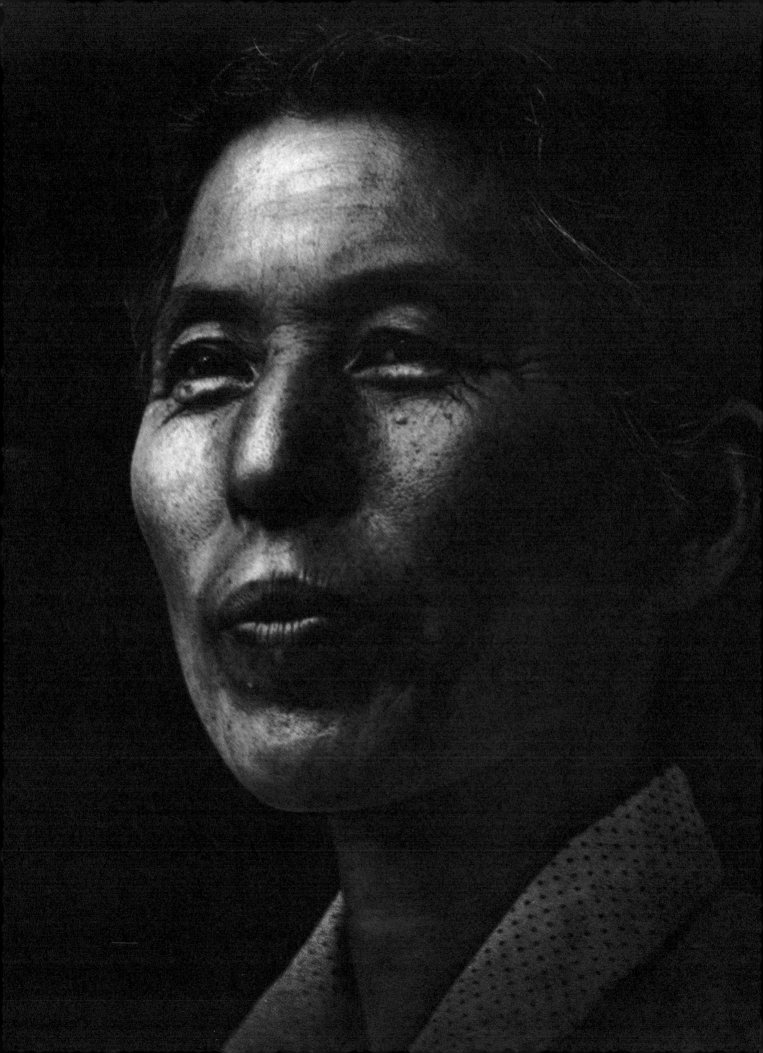

◁ Face of toil.

outside is white with snow. A god shelf (*kamidana*) in the *tatami* room still holds a miniature shrine that is used in daily worship. Throughout Japan, Shinto shrines still hear the voices of many, though the central meaning of the faith has evaporated with the loss of belief in the divine emperor.

The new generation pays little heed. Shinto celebrations are practiced more as tradition than as serious religious ceremonies. Many people remain atheists. Christianity has made meager progress, with only 2% of the population embracing the faith. Radical changes are for the young, and quite naturally, the Japanese are ready to reach out for anything that seems to offer rapid improvement and stability—solutions for their immediate problems. For this reason, *Soka Gakkai*, an energetic but intolerant philosophy, is currently claiming an alarming number of converts among the

海ほうずき

new generation. Oh, for a faith based on love and understanding that will once again give this valiant people a firm foundation.

Despite all this, the young people are a happy lot. Better economic conditions and the availability of more jobs are challenges to their growing desires and aspirations. On holidays, the beaches are crowded with merrymakers. No spot in Japan is far from the seashore. Shellfish stands and novelty shops abound. For a few yen, children can buy a string of dried fish egg cases. These are noise makers, emitting a rasping sound when little mouths force air through them. A kind of sweet treat is a steamed bean bun called *manju*. Shell rings and necklaces appeal to the children, while wooden trays inlaid with tiny shells are attractive souvenirs.

A circle of hysterically laughing young people means that a watermelon contest is in progress on

Winding trolley line — Enoshima.

the beach. The blindfolded subject is spun around several times and then left on his own. If he can cut a gash in the watermelon with a single stroke of the stick it becomes his prize. (*Color plates,* 16, 17.)

From Fujisawa, an old streetcar winds slowly between the hills, passing numerous villages where thatch-roofed houses cling to the steep hillsides. Clattering wheels sing their familiar song. The car emerges, from time to time, at a high point where passengers will see a magnificent view of the Pacific. In the afternoon these cars are crowded with chattering youngsters of all ages returning from school, each in his black and white uniform. Pent-up energies burst forth in laughter and pranks. In wet weather the same happy faces peer from beneath a brigade of colorful umbrellas. Children every-where are the same, and we—we are just older children.

70

During Gion Festival in Kyoto, merrymakers gather at riverside restaurants after sundown.

かまくら

At the end of the trolley ride is the town of Kamakura. A number of impressive shrines remind the visitor that Kamakura was capital of Japan in the dim past (1192-1333). A warm Sunday afternoon brings a crowd of strollers (*Color plate* 19) to visit these attractions, along with merchants who display their wares on temporary stands, much like the vendors in New York's Central Park. Nearby, a hopeful merchant spreads his stock of paintings and scrolls on the ground. (*Color plate* 20.) Along the broad stone avenue leading to Hachiman Shrine, shops exhibit artware and shells. Interspersed among these are small restaurants where vinegared rice, curried rice, and iced noodles tempt the appetite. As the continuous procession of visitors climbs the extraordinarily long flight of steps to the shrine, a very young artist works intently on her drawing of the structure. A proud father watches patiently. (*Color plate* 22.) On the corner a group of priests with shaven heads stands in the shade for a moment's rest. (*Color plate* 18.)

74

京の職人

Much of the pottery offered for sale in Kamakura, and indeed throughout Japan, comes from the city of Kyoto, where one of the oldest arts in Japan thrives. Methods are much the same today as they were centuries ago. Some of the world's finest ceramic ware and *cloisonne* come from this area. In ancient Japan, such craftsmen occupied the lowest position on the social ladder, even below the farmers. Though they are regarded more highly today, many still fare badly in the task of making a living.

One shop displays row after row of intricately decorated ceramic goods. A narrow stairway leads to a dark and poorly ventilated room where much of the work is done. Skilled fingers of a young worker turn out vases and bowls on the pottery wheel with such astonishing speed that it almost seems like sleight of hand. A thin figure, hard at work, squats in the corner where a single bulb

76

清水寺

provides all the illumination. The hollow-chested craftsman patiently applies detailed decoration to one of a mountain of vases that surrounds him. Within reach is a *hibachi* where his pot of tea is kept warm. Long hours, stale air, inadequate light, poor pay . . . meager rewards for skill.

Kyoto, capital of Japan until 1869, abounds in fascinating structures that tell a story of long ago. Often erected in choice locations on high knolls, Shinto shrines and Buddhist temples dominate the landscape. Despite the fact that the sects and cults they represent are very old, few of the present buildings are older than three or four hundred years. Earthquakes and fires have been a continuous menace in a land where nearly everything is built of wood.

Looking out over the city from its protective location on a steep hill, Kiyomizu Temple is a mammoth but not very decorative structure.

78

Almost entirely unpainted, the main building is supported by timbers and columns of immense size. Some of these, two or three feet in diameter, weigh nearly two tons. One can still hear echoes of groans and sighs where sweaty workmen strained to move the giant timbers up the hill and lift them into position. Here stands their work, a link with the past—a tribute to hands that toiled and to hearts that believed.

The interior of the temple is a broad expanse of floor broken only by several rows of columns, and open to the outside on three sides. A great wooden drum resting on an enormous pillow is placed to one side of the altar. Smoke curls up lazily from a square box of sand supporting dozens of sticks of smoldering incense. A group of worshippers, now on their knees, have placed the incense in remembrance of the dead for whom they pray. A priest with shaven head leads the service. (*Color plates* 23, 24.)

In contrast to Kiyomizu Temple, Chion-in Temple, just a short distance away, has a most elaborate interior. Gold leaf is used everywhere, enough of it to pave a street. Wood surfaces are lacquered red and green. Chion-in is one of the largest temples in Japan, the present building having been erected in 1633. It is headquarters for the Jodo sect of Buddhism, founded in 1211. (*Color plate* 26.) The ultimate aspiration of members is to be reborn in the Jodo (Pure land) in order to enjoy happiness after death by relying upon faith in him. Believers have to recite, day and night, the prayer formula, *Namu-Amida-Butsu*, as many times as possible.

But not all places of worship are built on this scale. Thousands of simple wayside Shinto shrines dot the countryside. Standing before the altar, the worshipper claps his hands three times and bows low, the bow being held as long as possible to

impress the spirits. An offering of food and drink is usually presented to the deity enshrined. Such offerings are of great importance, for they provide spiritual nourishment. The more vivid and sublime the expression of address, the greater its appeal to the god. Far more stress, therefore, is laid on the formality of the prayer than its content. The worshipper asks for a successful day, a safe journey or perhaps freedom from some affliction.

Young and old alike are attracted to annual village festivals such as the one at Karasumori. Women in gay kimonos plod along the dusty country road with children strapped upon their backs. From all around they come to join in the festivities. The older people move slowly, for the day is hot. One old woman squats by the roadside to enjoy a long cigar.

村まつり

Festival at Karasumori. ▷
Top right, false faces.
Top left, grandmother's treat.
Bottom, young explorer wandering.

At first the celebration looks very much like a carnival, for there are many stands selling cotton candy, cold drinks, toy windmills, and other novelties. It is, however, a Shinto celebration for the god of the local shrine. A cart decorated with flags is pulled up to the gate. Inside are musicians who will play for the deity. Children crowd the stands searching for a gaily colored hat or a sparkling bracelet. Rows of plastic funny faces attract the youngsters, who giggle with delight.

Towards the end of the day people gather before the shrine where Shinto priests do a ceremonial dance. The god has been good to his people this year. He is to be praised and thanked for his goodness, and perhaps he will continue to smile upon the village. Here is a glimpse into the distant past, a tradition as old as Japan itself.

84

Attired in clothing appropriate for a Shinto festival, an old farmer is fatigued by the relentless merrymaking.

Among the special annual Buddhist celebrations is the Festival of the Dead (July 13-15). On the first day, newly woven mats are spread upon all Buddhist altars. Decorations of lotus blossoms and colored paper are hung. Food offerings consisting of *gozen*, or boiled rice, *dango*, a tiny dumpling, eggplant, and fruit are placed upon a lacquered table at the altar. Tea is poured every hour for the

Ice cream and cotton candy.

invisible visitors. The dead feast in this manner over the entire three-day period. At night, relatives of the dead visit the cemeteries, where they make offerings, pray, and burn incense. Beneath the light of many lanterns, water is poured for the ghosts, and flowers are placed in bamboo vases. On the third night, *toro-nagashi* concludes the festival. Paper lanterns on floats are prepared by priests and sold, depending on their size, for 50 to 500 yen.

88

In the evening the lanterns are lighted and set afloat on the river in memory of the dead. A tender prayer for the departed soul goes with them. If the lantern is overturned and its light extinguished, the prayer will not reach the loved one. The unusual display is fascinating to watch, for hundreds of tiny lights shimmer and dance in the river. Slowly the lanterns float out to sea, carried by the current, with their messages for the land beyond.

At the edge of the small city of Tamashima is a steep hill, dense with pines. From the base of the hill ancient stone steps begin an ascent that twists and turns like a restless serpent as it runs between houses huddled together. The heavy stones are cracked and worn, here and there sinking almost out of sight into the ground. The ascent grows ever steeper, and soon the houses are left behind. A decaying Buddhist cemetery appears on the right, where pine branches nearly obscure the tilted

stones. One shudders and hesitates, almost expecting to see a phantom from a time long past standing on the timeless steps. In the cool shade of dense pines and bamboos stand row after row of tombstones, crowded together with only inches between. All are chipped and mouldered and mossed, marks of the centuries that have flown so quickly by. Through vaulted foliage the sunlight leaks to warm the green moss in patches of thin light.

Tall, slender wooden laths, standing in places as thick as young bamboos, rise from the black soil among the stones. Each is painted with Japanese characters on both sides. One inscription reads "To promote Buddhahood." Immediately beneath is recorded the dead person's name. The other surface always contains a Sanskrit sentence whose meaning has been lost in the dim corridors of time. When the monument is first erected, one lath is planted directly behind it. Another is planted

every seven days for forty-nine days; then one after 100 days; one at the end of the year; one more after three years; and so on over successively longer periods for 100 years. Some of the strips of wood are black with age. Others lay forgotten in the soil where they fell long years before.

In accordance with ancient Buddhist beliefs, adult dead are attired in white, and a wallet is placed about the neck. In the wallet are three coins, the price that must be paid to cross the phantom River of the Three Roads (Sanzu-no-Kawa). In that world of ghosts, an old woman, ghastly and gray as in some nightmare, waits at the bank. From those souls unable to pay she takes away their clothes, which she hangs upon the trees.

Where the path opens out into the light, three stone figures stand in the tall grass. Two of these, with childlike faces, smile faintly. They are images of Jizo, the most beautiful and tender figure

Worn and broken by the centuries, stone figures of the gentle Jizo still bear a trace of a smile as they guard dead children in the Sai-no-Kawara.

95

三途の川

in Japanese Buddhist faith. It is this divinity who cares for the souls of little children, protecting them from demons in the place of unrest. One figure holds a Buddhist incense box. The second, whose clasped hands have been worn and broken off, stands in an attitude of prayer. Remains of a cotton garment hang loosely about his shoulders. Each statue is surrounded by piles of small stones, and the stones are piled upon the folded arms and sometimes even upon the head; for the child-ghosts build little towers of stones for penance in the Sai-no-Kawara. Demons frighten and torment the children and throw down the stone piles they build. Jizo comes to calm the babes and hide them in his great sleeves. The demons are sternly sent away. Mothers of dead children pray to Jizo and heap the stones at his feet to help the little ones in their shadowy existence.

The path goes on, and one wonders to what antique and mysterious relic of old Japan it may lead. Around the final bend, where wind-blown pines

96

Plate 21   A quiet smoke.

Plate 22   A young artist pauses for a moment's reflection as she sketches on the great stone steps of Hachiman Shrine —Kamakura.

Plates 23, 24
Pious Buddhists participate in service led by priest with shaven head—Kiyomizu Temple, Kyoto.

Plate 25
Bridge at Enoshima.

Plate 26   The pond, Chion-in Temple—Kyoto.

Plate 27   Ancient Buddhist stone images—Tamashima.

Plate 28   Beggar seeks food at each shop—Kurashiki.

Plate 29   Buddhist font: wooden slats bear names of the dead for
            whom a prayer has been said.

Plate 30   Merrymakers gather at gaily lighted riverside restaurants
            during festival at Kyoto.

Plate 31   *Reflections on a rainy night—Kyoto.*

Plate 33   Beach scene—Kotsubo.

◀ Plate 32   Kotsubo sunrise.

Plate 34   Sankei-en gardens—Yokohama.

Plate 35   Nets—Kotsubo.

Plate 36
Stately Fuji, riding in a sea of clouds, stands guard as generations come and go—Kotsubo beach.

Plate 37   Ageless stone lanterns, draped in moss, are silent sentinels in the Tokugawa Mausoleo—Nikko.

Plate 40   An oriental sunset. ▶

Plates 38, 39   The Karamon Gate at Nikko.   *Plate 41*   **Shinto god.** ▶

assume grotesque and twisted shapes, a final sharp ascent opens into a forest clearing. There in peaceful solitude stands a structure with heavy thatched roof. It is Entsuji Temple. To the right of the approach a crude wooden shelter protects another group of Buddhist stone images. (*Color plate* 27.)

If the visitor strikes a wooden gong, a priest appears to open the temple doors. Shoes are left outside; floors are *tatami* mat. Within the main sanctuary, gold lotus blossoms gleam in the dim light. They stand in vases on either side of the altar. The air is thick with mystery, and a feeling of awe overcomes the viewer. For centuries Buddhist scholars worked here seeking harmony with the universe and peace of soul. Here the prayers and wishes of many now sealed in their tombs were heard—prayers so insignificant to us these long years later once came from passionate hearts and quivering lips. To this sacred ground came those who asked for victory against the Russian armies in 1904. Perhaps from this very spot one could have

△ *High priest*

◁ *Entsuji Temple — Tamashima.*

The wisdom of Buddha. ▷

Priest's private quarters were quiet hours
▽ are spent in prayer and meditation.

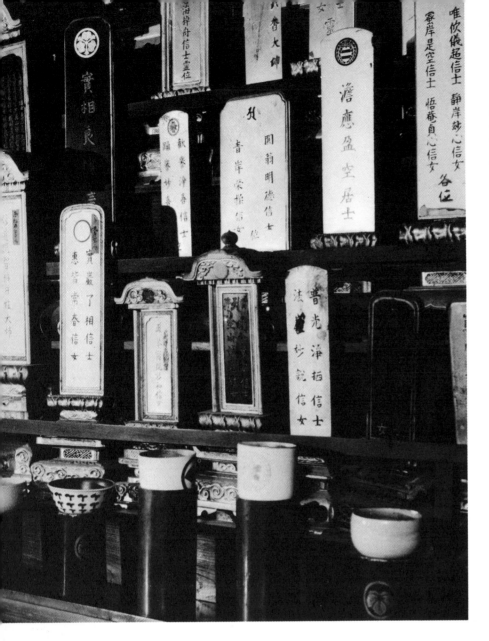

Row upon row of gold plaques fill the sacred inner room of Entsuji Temple. Each plaque is inscribed with the Buddhist name of a loved one who has passed on.

seen the blinding flash that carried many thousands into eternity at Hiroshima not far away.

Eyes accustom themselves slowly to the dim light within, where gold plaques in memory of the dead stand in neat, long rows. At the far end of the room is the priest's private prayer booth. An iron lantern emits a wan light. Through a door to the sacred garden, a stone cistern can be seen with its bamboo-handled cup. (*Color plate* 29.) Before holy meditation, worshippers stop to purify hands and soul.

118

A short distance from Entsuji, the path reaches the crest of the hill and suddenly presents a breathtaking view. One looks out upon a broad expanse of blue water dotted with tiny islands. In the distance, so faint as to merge with the horizon, a long range of mountains separates sea and sky. It rises from the island of Shikoku, and the expanse of water between is known as Seto-naikai, Japan's inland sea. Small fishing craft glide silently over the

The Pacific laps volcanic shores at Kotsubo.

Nightfall; a single lantern plays upon still waters.

小坪の朝

tranquil waters as if on the surface of a mirror. It is a study in subtle tones where every glance surprises the eye with new discoveries. At this moment one seems to share the thoughts of an endless procession of painters whose work sings of love for their homeland.

The very great length of their sea coast has made the Japanese a seafaring nation. From primitive times they have depended upon the sea for food. Destruction of a large part of the fishing fleet during World War II brought about a serious shortage, for rice and fish form the bulk of the diet. Even today the catch does not equal that of the pre-war period.

The shores are dotted with tiny fishing villages, where life proceeds much as it did a century ago. Nearly hidden by steep cliffs that are thrust up abruptly from the Pacific floor, Kotsubo is a picture

122

A bountiful catch is taken ashore by barefooted fishermen.

of the simple life. Struggling for a foothold on the precipitous hills, much of the tiny village appears ready to slide into the sea. A steady low roar is heard where swirling waters have carved out subterranean caves.

From twisted metal chimneys, thin blue smoke curls lazily into the chill air. Here and there, paper windows are slid open to the cool morning air as the populace begins to stir. In the distance a dim gray frame of peaks rides upon a spectral sea. Faintly tinted vaporous clouds send nebulous fingers between each knoll and clump of pines, which take fire with touches of violet and gold in the glory of the Japanese morning. (*Color plate* 32.) And now a flood of warm light fills the valley, penetrating the delicious haze as the sun's rim appears. Dark volcanic sand forms a short beach where deep red clumps of seaweed are strewn at high tide. Today the ocean is calm; the breeze is brisk.

124

Preparing the nets—Kotsubo. △

The great cloud—Kotsubo. ▷

Ready to put to sea. △

Setting octopus traps. ▷

たこつぼ

Boiling shirasu on the beach. ▷

On the beach, nets are being prepared by women protected from the scorching sun by a canvas canopy. Children frolic at the water's edge, drawing designs in the sand.

Several men tie heavy earthenware jars together to be used as octopus traps. They will be sunk to the ocean floor, where the tentacled marauders of the deep, thinking them to be empty shells, will try to make homes of them. To the west, the peak of Mt. Fuji rides above billowy clouds like a mirage in the sky. The extinct volcano is forty miles from Kotsubo. (*Color plate* 36.)

Women scurry to the beach when the boats return, and wading into the surf, help remove the catch in baskets. Suntanned backs gleam with sweat as young helpers turn the sweeping arms of the winch that pulls the fishing craft safely onto the beach. With the numerous varieties of larger fish, the waters yield a bulk of tiny *shirasu*. These fish, about an inch in length, are boiled on the spot in

vats over a wood fire. The cooked fish are spread on mats to dry in the sun, where they look like endless rows of white crabmeat.

At sundown, when the day's work is done, fishing boats stand in ranks, secured until the new day dawns. The beach is deserted.

Long ago, when the islands of Japan were young and the gods still dwelt on earth, the fierce sea dragon made off with the emperor's precious

stone and took it to the bottom of the sea. But three items of the emperor's regalia were most important: a mirror, a wondrous sword, and the precious stone; the stone had to be recovered. The emperor's sister agreed to swim to the depths

Sea dragon. △

◁　*Dragon.*

where the monster dwelt and bring it back.
Finding the dragon away, she snatched up the stone,
and with utmost haste moved toward the surface.
But the dragon discovered his loss and set out in
pursuit.　Naturally a sea monster can quickly over-
take even the most powerful swimmer.　Knowing
that the dragon's only dislike is human blood, the
princess cut a deep gash beneath her left breast and
held the jewel close to the wound as she swam with
all her strength.　When she reached the surface the
stone was safe, but there she breathed her last.

　　Japanese legend contains countless stories about
the dragon.　Some of these originate in earlier
Chinese literature.　Among other things, the mean
old fellow seems to be concerned with the weather,
and is responsible for great storms and typhoons.
But he has been of service, too.　Centuries ago,
when Japan was under attack from the Asian mainland, the dragon blew up a fierce typhoon that
destroyed the invading fleet.

Along the canal in Kurashiki houses built by another generation live proudly into the modern age.

The town of Kurashiki in western Honshu is totally untouched by the ravages of the great war. In its older sections, frail houses crowd the unpaved streets. Though brighter color schemes are slowly being adopted from the west, the Japanese prefer natural wood colors, and most houses are unpainted. Pine, cedar, and bamboo yield tasteful variations of tone and texture.

Where shops abound, the narrow streets are spanned with awnings, and bicyclists pedal in all directions. Noisy carts bump past, raising a cloud of dust as they go. A beggar in burlap rags makes his way from door to door, entreating each shopkeeper to provide a handout. Sometimes young Buddhist priests practice this same ritual, begging alms as a part of their training.

Through Kurashiki runs a very old canal. It is spanned at several points by arched bridges. Graceful willows bend low to touch its lazy waters. Once

138

Where the lotus blooms.

*Cobblestones and stovepipes,
the older section — Kurashiki.*

Business district — Kurashiki.

Raindrops in a sleeping garden—Kurashiki.

this canal was an important artery, for it connects the commercial area with the Inland Sea. Barges laden with wares of many merchants traversed its now quiet waters. A quaint inn stands where a great stone lantern marks a sharp bend in the canal. The charming garden of the Kurashiki Ryokan (inn) makes the heart thrill with the beauty of this ancient art. Dwarfed plants and small stone lanterns are arranged against a background of large trees and curiously shaped stones. Often an island set in a lake and connected with the mainland by arched bridges provides the theme. There is little trace of artificiality.

Unlike the abominations sometimes found in the west, the Japanese landscape garden is a delicate work of art. It is not primarily a flowering garden, and indeed may contain no flowering plants at all. Its purpose is to recreate a portion of nature complete with the sensations of joy, solemnity, and peace that nature alone can arouse. In a volcanic

142

land, where shapes in stone are most suggestive to the imagination, stones form an important part of these landscape designs. To fully appreciate the beauty of the gardens, one must learn to understand the beauty of stones.

At dusk the eight foot-tall lantern illuminates the gravel path. Through low-hanging branches the inn is outlined against a darkening sky. Paper doors are aglow with a soft mellow light. Here the traveller may spend the night. Hostesses in kimonos bring hot tea and a damp cloth to freshen tired faces and hands. A steaming hot bath is prepared where one can soak and relax. The Japanese bath is deeper but shorter than the western-style tub. Several people may use the same water. Since one soaps and rinses before getting in to soak, the water is kept surprisingly clean.

Rooms are equipped with hanging scrolls, pillows, a low table, and little else. Paper doors make up the entire outside wall, and beyond them is the charming garden. When it is time to retire,

soft quilts are spread two deep on the *tatami* floor, much as a camper would do with his sleeping bag. The tired traveller may look on in dismay, but he finds the Japanese bed comfortable. It has the added advantage of easy storage, to save space during the daytime.

Now in the dark all is quiet, save for the steady trickle of gentle rain outside. A lantern creaks as it swings in its hook. Nodding pine branches cast

146

changing abstract patterns on the paper door panels. How many, long ago, watched these dancing silhouettes and heard the fragile sound of raindrops in a sleeping garden? This is Japan—beautiful, geniune, unmatched. It lives not in words, but in the heart, returning in quiet moments to set thoughts ablaze. How many from some distant time are linked with us by moments of beauty such as these, where time has no meaning?

Some of man's finest handiwork is found in the mausolea erected in Nikko for the founders of the Tokugawa Shogunate. The buildings, completed in 1636, represent one of Japan's most important national treasures. The finest artists and craftsmen were summoned from all over Japan at government expense to blend their skills. About two and a half million sheets of gold leaf went into the construction, enough to cover six acres. Man and nature vie for attention. The setting is as unique and colossal

as the buildings erected here. Steep mountains, azure blue lakes, and dozens of waterfalls delight the eye. Thriving forests present a wide variety of plant life to the botanist. Over three hundred years ago, long avenues of cedar trees were planted here; now these erect giants rise to dizzy heights.

Probably the most elaborate and important shrine in this area is the Toshogu shrine, containing the tomb of Ieyasu Tokugawa. The approach is a broad flight of stone steps spanned by a huge granite *torii*. Standing 27 feet six inches high, it is the largest stone torii in Japan. In the early days, the lower classes were not allowed inside the temple, but were permitted to assemble on these steps beneath the torii.

Priests with broad sun hats are dwarfed beside the Yomeimon Gate (Gate of Sunlight). This piece of architecture, considered by many to be the most beautiful gate in Japan, is so elaborate that one can

148

Here dwell the Shinto gods. ▷

scarcely find an uncarved section anywhere. It is popularly called the Gate of Twilight, implying that one wishes to inspect it until overtaken by twilight.

Beyond it, the Karamon Gate (Chinese Gate) opens into the oratory and chief edifices of the Shrine. A fantastic bronze animal stands guard on the front gable of the gate, and dragons appear on either side. (*Color plates* 37, 38, 39.) Japanese apricots, chrysanthemums, and bamboos stand in relief on the carved doors. A fairy playing a harp decorates the ceiling, and below her are a series of Chinese figures. One marvels at their excellent condition, despite their age, and has the awesome sensation that time has suddenly turned back 300 years.

Matted branches of tall cedars close out the sky like thick gathering clouds. On toward the tomb the air grows chill and damp. Patches of moss trim stone lanterns with a cushion of bright green.

ゆめうつつ

Water oozes from cracks in a towering wall that holds back the forest. Fanlike ferns rise from the dark soil. (*Color plate* 37.)

But what is this? The silence is broken by distant voices. Shadowy figures in procession appear and disappear through the trees. Somewhere a mournful bell is tolling. Now the slow solemn chant of deep voices is unmistakable. A funeral? It cannot be—the mausoleum has been closed for centuries. Its wooden gates near the tomb are etched and splintered by rain and ice. Stone walls lean and bulge where restless movements of earth have done their slow but constant work. One blinks and peers again, unsure of sound and sight. Through deep shadows the sombre procession moves. Like phantoms in some macabre half-dream, its members wearily plod along as if they had marched on forever through time. And now the casket can be seen. The shogun is dead . . . *the shogun is dead.* The mind trembles and rejects the

152

The bell.

thought; there is no shogun in our time. Can it be that this ghost train brings the last remains of Tokugawa Ieyasu to the tomb?

It was Ieyasu who established a firm rule by the final defeat of the Toyotomis at Osaka Castle. It was he who organized the feudal social order that remained until the opening of Japan to the outside world. Sure enough, colored robes identify the *kuge* (court nobles) walking before the casket. A group of *buke* (warriors) with sheathed swords follow. Forbidden to enter the inner oratory, townsmen and farmers peer through the lower gate. Two foreigners in the procession who seem to be Dutch merchants in the attire of the Middle Ages set the heart to pounding, for it now appears certain that some sinister force has transported us in a fleeting moment back through the centuries.

The procession moves out of sight, leaving an awesome silence. Is this 1965 or 1636? Can it be the mind playing tricks? Was it all a fantasy or

154

静寂の墓

could it have been real? In panic the eye searches the route taken by the strange procession. There is no sign of life. Moss on the cobblestone pathway is undisturbed. The red lacquered corridor bears no footprints. The long stairway is silent and empty. And there at its end is the tomb, its great bronze door sealed forever—sealed in the distant past. Along the pathway silent rocks hold their secret fast. For them time has no meaning. Little do they know of aging mortals who pass them by in never-ending parade.

A welcome beam of sunlight penetrates the trees and warms the face. Now the mind struggles to clear. A bird circles overhead. The familiar rustle of leaves returns. Shadows on the mossed tree trunks cast by dancing branches mimic movements of the apparition. Could it have been these shadows that played upon the already pregnant imagination? Beyond the walled enclosure, voices of other visitors to the Shrine can now be heard.

For we are here but a fleeing moment
to walk the earth, then pass again to
dust. Yet in that moment each leaves
a mark, indelible, distinct—the seed
from which the future springs.

157

Classes of happy schoolchildren gather to see the famous structure built for the Tokugawas. Into this modern age, confused by a still indigestible mixture of east and west, they move and have their being. Only in another dimension can they strengthen the gossamer thread linking them with their ancestors. Beside the towering shrine gate a great hand firmly clasps the hilt of a drawn sword. With savage expression and penetrating eyes the Shinto gods faithfully stand guard for those who, in life, molded the Japan of long, long ago. (*Color plate* 41.) And as the people stroll, perhaps for some the phantom procession will choose to pass again.

In a world of facts and realities, where the seen and the unseen, the material and the spiritual, seldom find a happy meeting place, we have dared to build a bridge. Its timbers are the trestles of the

158

さよなら

mind, which transcend time. It leads beyond the
reality of the present to wherever the thoughts
would roam. And when we cross our fragile bridge
in search of moments lost in time, who can say we
were not there . . . in old Japan?

A NOTE ON THE ILLUSTRATIONS

The Photographs

All photography in this publication was done with the Mamiyaflex C-2 2¼″ square twin lens reflex camera. Lenses employed were the normal 80mm and the 180mm telephoto.

The black and white photographs were made on Kodak Professional Plus-X Pan film and processed in Microdol-X. Professional Ektachrome film was employed for the color work.

Because I always try to avoid the harshness of single flash wherever possible, only one flash picture appears in this collection—The Pottery Wheel on page 75. One has to travel as light as possible when constantly on the move, and the transport of more bulky multiple flash equipment is difficult.

A number of the pictures have had special work done on them. One of these appears on page 31. On the original negative the aged figure is shuffling along in front of a row of houses. Despite the interesting figure, a straight print proved to be unsatisfactory as a piece of art, for the background was distracting, the lighting was flat, and there was a lack of emotional appeal. The surroundings were therefore removed by chemical reduction. After painting in the streaks of rain and the reflections with designer's black watercolor paint, I rephotographed the result and printed the new negative through a Japanese paper of selected texture to produce this finished semi-abstract design.

The Art Work

All pencil sketches were done on the spot, some on a relatively smooth surfaced drawing paper, and others on Cameo paper (clay surfaced). For the watercolors, I employed Talens pigments on d'Arches paper.

Like many watercolorists, I prefer to do my painting indoors from thumbnail sketches that contain the necessary color notations. Watercolor is a sensitive medium that is made more difficult to control by the hot sun that dries out the paper and the breeze that blows grit into the paints. It is, however, a real pleasure to work on the spot with pencil. Groups of chattering youngsters often collected to watch as I sketched. Occasionally I was driven under cover by frequent showers that come especially during the early part of the summer throughout Japan.

Though I work in other media too, pencil and watercolor are my favorites. They are also most practical when travelling, requiring very little equipment. Pastels are far too fragile, while oils require too much time in execution and also in drying.

MORTON WESLEY HUBER